LOUISVILLE
The Delaplaine
2020
Long Weekend Guide

No business listed in this guide has provided *anything* free to be included.

Andrew Delaplaine

Senior Editors - ***Renee & Sophie Delaplaine***
Senior Writer - **James Cubby**

Gramercy Park Press
New York London Paris

Copyright © by Gramercy Park Press - All rights reserved.

Please submit corrections, additions or comments to
andrewdelaplaine@mac.com

LOUISVILLE
The Delaplaine Long Weekend Guide

TABLE OF CONTENTS

Chapter 1 – WHY LOUISVILLE? – 4

Chapter 2 – GETTING ABOUT – 8

Chapter 3 – WHERE TO STAY – 9
High on the Hog – Sensible Alternatives – Budget

Chapter 4 – WHERE TO EAT – 19
Extravagant – Middle Ground – Budget

Chapter 5 – NIGHTLIFE – 45

Chapter 6 – WHAT TO SEE & DO – 52

Chapter 7 – SHOPPING & SERVICES – 69

INDEX – 75

OTHER BOOKS BY THE SAME AUTHOR – 79

Chapter 1
WHY LOUISVILLE?

If you follow the booze industry, or even hang out in semi-fashionable bars and lounges anywhere in the world, you can't have escaped the realization that bourbon has become one of the hottest categories in the spirits business.

Kentucky is the Bourbon Capital of the World, and within the Bluegrass State, the epicenter of all this activity is Louisville. People come here before they go out into the hinterlands to visit the distilleries. (Actually, the town of Bardstown, about 40 minutes from Louisville, trademarked the term "Bourbon Capital of the World," but that's hair-splitting.)

The amount of bourbon selling each year goes up greater than any other spirit. Sales will top $5 billion shortly. Production of the liquor has jumped 50% just over the last decade.

If you added up all the barrels currently aging in Louisville distilleries, the number would be greater than the number of people that live in the state, and for that matter, the number of horses, *combined!*

Now, that's a lot of bourbon.

A great deal of the increase in bourbon shipments has been to foreign countries, places like Dubai, Singapore, Tokyo, where a taste for bourbon has become all the rage among the moneyed elites in these countries. The greatest growth has come within the super premium categories.

As sales have soared against other segments of the liquor industry (vodka, tequila, gin, Scotch), the so-called Big Six distilleries (including Jim Beam, Heaven Hill, Brown-Forman, Wild Turkey, Four Roses and Diageo) have ramped up production.

The new keen interest from consumers has proved strong enough to encourage numerous entrepreneurs to launch craft distilleries. And while the Big Six still gobble up sales, accounting for some 90%, there's room enough for these craft distilleries to make a dent because they tend to produce only high-end, handcrafted bourbons that are highly prized.

All these factors have led to an increase in tourism for Louisville and the rest of the state. Tourists visiting distilleries passed the 500,000 mark recently, and the numbers keep rising.

Along with all this attention, the indie foodie scene in Louisville has exploded, with great new restaurants popping up every week.

But it's not all about bourbon in Louisville. The city has a fascinating history, made even more notable by what happens the first Saturday in May.

That marks the annual running of the Kentucky Derby, of course. It was conceived in 1872 when Col. Meriwether Lewis Clark Jr. (grandson of the Lewis & Clark Expedition's William Clark) returned from a European tour having attended the English Derby and the Grand Prix de Paris at the famous racetrack Longchamps.

Once back home, he put together the Louisville Jockey Club and raised money to build a track. (The track gets its name from brothers Henry and John Churchill, who contributed the land for the track.) It's been run every year since 1875.

It's been called "The Most Exciting Two Minutes In Sports," and I've always wondered what brilliant PR guy came up with that stupendous moniker. It sounds like hype, but if you've ever seen the Kentucky Derby, you'll realize it's not hype at all. It really is the most exciting two minutes in sports. The

Derby record is still held by Secretariat, who ran the race in 1:59.

The race is 1 ¼ miles long. The Derby is the first race in the Triple Crown. After the Derby, the second leg is the Preakness Stakes in Baltimore (at 1 3/16 miles), following by the Belmont Stakes (at 1 ½ miles).

The city fathers have been trying to create more of a year-round tourist city out of Louisville, and the bourbon industry seems to be aiding this goal. As I said above, the interesting food scene is helping as well.

After the Downtown area, you'll want to explore **Highlands** for its excellent shopping. This is on **Bardstown Road** (from around Broadway down to the Douglass Loop) where you'll find a wide variety of cafés, upscale restaurants, art galleries, lots of bars (some great dives as well).

You hear all kinds of weird pronunciations of the town's name. You even hear the god-awful "Lewisville," which is so wrong. Then there's *LOOey-vil* and *LOOuh-vuhl* and *LU-vuhl*.

In my opinion, the best way is: *LOOuh-vuhl.*

Chapter 2
GETTING ABOUT

You will only need a car if you venture far from Downtown, Highlands, Frankfort Avenue, Old Louisville. Everything is quite walkable. But you'll need a car to go anywhere else.

Use **Uber** or **Lyft** if you like. They can take you to the airport, but will not pick you up there. (Legal hassles.) Use them to get around town if you don't want to rent a car.

There's a bus system, **TARC**, that is all right. Buses now have bike racks and there's an aggressive program to make the roads even more bike-friendly than they already are.

Get the bus schedule here - www.ridetarc.org

Chapter 3
WHERE TO STAY

21c MUSEUM HOTEL
700 West Main St, Louisville, 502-217-6300
www.21chotel.com
Located in historic downtown Louisville, this hotel that opened in 2006 (in an area of old tobacco warehouses that were restored) is a unique combination of a 90-room boutique hotel with a contemporary art museum, an award-winning locally-sourced restaurant and a civic center.

This is a most interesting place, a destination all by itself, really, because of the "museum" aspect of the property, which commissions site-specific works and curated dynamic group and solo exhibitions, which are free to the public and open every day of the year. Owners Laura Lee Brown and Steve Wilson display not only their own art, but others' as well. By opening the place, they insure a steady stream of local customers.

With all this art around, the bar and restaurant are naturally filled with the local creative types that make Louisville so interesting. The restaurant, **Proof on Main**, was named one the Best Restaurants in the country by "Esquire." The bar here carries over 50 Kentucky bourbons.

Guest rooms and suites offer spacious accommodations and a comfortable respite from all the activity that fills the museum. Amenities include: Original art, 42 HDTV flat screen TVs with full cable, luxurious bedding, pewter mint julep cups, and free high speed Wi-Fi.

BRECKINRIDGE INN
2800 Breckinridge Ln, Louisville, 502-456-5050
www.breckinridgeinn.com
This traditional southern inn features 123 tastefully decorated, non-smoking guest rooms. Amenities include: Cable TV, free Wi-Fi, and free continental breakfast buffet. Hotel facilities include: indoor pool, seasonal outdoor pool, whirlpool, exercise room and tennis court. Conveniently located near attractions

like Churchill Downs and the Louisville Zoo. Free airport shuttle.

BROWN HOTEL
335 West Broadway, Louisville, 888-888-5252
www.brownhotel.com
Home of the original "**Hot Brown**," this historic AAA Four Diamond luxury hotel (dating back to 1923) offers beautiful accommodations and boasts the reputation as one of the finest hotels in the South. The opulent two-story lobby greets guests with its beautiful marble floors, hand-painted, coffered ceiling and Palladian-style windows. The bar in the lobby is another big local hangout. Amenities include: European goose down duvets, feather beds, flat-screen TVs and free high-speed Internet access. The Brown is known for its in-house restaurant, the **<u>English Grill</u>**. Conveniently located next to the

Brown Theatre and close to the Palace Theatre, 4th Street Live, and other local attractions.

THE DUPONT MANSION BED & BREAKFAST
1317 South Fourth St, Louisville, 502-638-0045
www.dupontmansion.com
Located in historic Old Louisville, this beautiful B&B is one of the finest inns in Kentucky. Beautifully restored, this 1884 Italian-style inn offers only 7 guest rooms with private baths, whirlpool tubs, and the amenities of a luxury hotel. Every morning a gourmet breakfast is served in the dining room. Free refreshments are served every evening. Amenities include: flat screen cable TV, electric fireplace inserts, luxury lines, and free wireless Internet service.

EMBASSY SUITES BY HILTON
9940 Corporate Campus Dry, Louisville, 502-426-9191
www.hilton.com/search/es/us/ky/louisville
This hotel offers spacious suites with separate living rooms. Amenities include: complimentary cooked-to-order breakfast, flat-screen TVs, and complimentary

Wi-Fi. Facility features include: an open-air atrium, indoor pool, whirlpool and fitness center. Conveniently located to attractions like Churchill Downs, Ox moor Mall and the Louisville Slugger Museum.

GALT HOUSE HOTEL
140 N 4th St, Louisville, 502-589-5200
www.galthouse.com
This is the largest hotel in Louisville with 1,300 guest rooms, including 650 suites. Amenities include: Wi-Fi (fee), flat screen HDTVs, and free shopping shuttle. Hotel features include: seasonal outdoor pool, salon, spa, 6 restaurants and lounges, and boutiques. Free Wi-Fi in public places. Non-smoking hotel.

HAMPTON INN LOUISVILLE DOWNTOWN
101 E Jefferson St, Louisville, 502-585-2200
www.hamptoninn3.hilton.com/
Modern hotel with 173 guest rooms typical of the Hampton Inn chain. Amenities include: free Wi-Fi, flat-screen TVs, coffeemakers and free hot breakfast and weekday breakfast bags to go. Suites have wet bars, minifridges and microwaves. Hotel features include: fitness center, indoor pool, and business center. Conveniently located near downtown attractions like the Louisville Slugger Factory and the entertainment district.

HYATT REGENCY LOUISVILLE
320 West Jefferson St, Louisville, 502-581-1234
https://louisville.regency.hyatt.com/en/hotel/home.html

True to the Hyatt name, this hotel offers spacious guestrooms and suites and a little dose of southern hospitality. Amenities include: flat screen TVs and Wi-Fi (fee). Hotel features include: 24-hour gym, outdoor tennis court, indoor pool, on-site restaurant/bar and a bagel shop. Conveniently located near Kentucky International Convention Center (with a direct connection to the hotel).

THE INN AT WOODHAVEN
401 S Hubbards Ln, Louisville, 502-895-1011
www.innatwoodhaven.com
NEIGHBORHOOD: St. Matthews
Built in 1853, this is one of the premier inns of Kentucky. The Inn, set on a lovely tree-lined street in a restful neighborhood, offers 8 elegantly furnished guest rooms all furnished with antiques and reproductions, four-poster beds and wing armchairs. In good weather, you can sit on the spacious front

porch and catch the breeze. Amenities: Complimentary breakfast and Wi-Fi, flat-screen TVs, mini-fridges, and coffeemakers. Facilities: 14 foot ceilings and floor to ceiling diamond paned windows. Some rooms feature whirlpool tubs, steam showers and/or fireplaces. Conveniently located near Louisville attractions, parks, fine dining and shopping areas.

SEELBACH HILTON HOTEL
500 S 4th St, Louisville, 502-585-3200
www.seelbachhilton.com
Built in 1905, it is considered a landmark to "the golden era" with its grand ambiance that inspired author F. Scott Fitzgerald to use the Seelbach as a backdrop for Tom and Daisy Buchanan's wedding in "The Great Gatsby." (The hotel even has a cameo in the movie.) And now a recent $12 million renovation

has taken this grand old hotel and combined it with all of the contemporary necessities. So now, you can not only experience genteel, Southern hospitality in historic grandeur. You can do so in updated guestrooms with new furniture, lighting and carpet while watching 37" hi-def televisions and taking advantage of high-speed Internet access. Fitness room, business center.

STAYBRIDGE SUITES LOUISVILLE EAST
11711 Gateworth Way, Louisville, 502-244-9511
Blankenbaker Pkwy & I-64 (Exit 17)
www.ihg.com/staybridge/hotels/us/en/louisville/sdfmt/hoteldetail
This extended stay hotel offers 94 guest rooms and suites. Amenities include: free continental breakfast, free Wi-Fi and cable TV. Hotel facilities include: outdoor pool, fitness center, laundry facilities, and business center.
Conveniently located near attractions like Renaissance Fun Park, Churchill Downs, and Maker's Mark Distillery.

Chapter 4
WHERE TO EAT

610 MAGNOLIA
610 W Magnolia Ave, Louisville, 502- 636-0783
www.610magnolia.com
CUISINE: Creative Southern
DRINKS: Full Bar

SERVING: Dinner Thursday-Saturday. Verify other days. Don't walk in. Book ahead.
PRICE RANGE: $$$$
NEIGHBORHOOD: Downtown
This is one of celebrated Chef Ed Lee's places. It's a small room with bricked flooring and bare-topped wooden tables. For a fine dining place, it's almost as if they wanted to go bare bones with the décor, but it's still quite nice with brightly colored art on the walls. Best idea here is to go for the Tasting Menu. It'll give you a feel for his inventive twist on Southern cooking. Expect items like smoked octopus; pan roasted lamb chop with shred leg of lamb; spiced catfish with bok choy; shaved fennel; lobster medallions; chicken thigh confit; pork osso bucco.

8UP
350 W Chestnut St, Louisville, 502-631-4180
www.8uplouisville.com/
CUISINE: American (New)
DRINKS: Full Bar
SERVING: Breakfast & Dinner
PRICE RANGE: $$
Trendy eatery featuring an eclectic menu popular with sophisticated guests and foodies. This 90-seat restaurant offers beautiful view of the city and an open kitchen so you can watch your meal being prepared. Popular nightlife spot. Open air rooftop bar. More of a scene than a dining establishment.

BLUE DOG BAKERY & CAFÉ
2868 Frankfort Ave, Louisville, 502-899-9800
www.bluedogbakeryandcafe.com/

CUISINE: Breakfast/Cafe
DRINKS: Full bar
SERVING: Breakfast & Lunch
PRICE RANGE: $$
NEIGHBORHOOD: Crescent Hill/The Avenue
Bakery/café offering a wide range of artisanal breads, croissants and muffins as well as delicious breakfast and lunch. Menu favorites: Breakfast pizza and French toast. Place gets crowded so there's often a wait.

BRENDON'S CATCH 23
505 S 4th St, Louisville, 502-909-3323
www.bcatch23.com
CUISINE: Steakhouse/Seafood
DRINKS: Full Bar
SERVING: Dinner; closed Sundays
PRICE RANGE: $$$
A high-end, chef driven restaurant offering a creative menu of seafood and steaks. Menu favorites include: Sea Bass & Scallops. Sophisticated dining at its best with large dining room, private dining rooms and cocktail bar known for its hand crafted cocktails.

BUTCHERTOWN GROCERY
1076 E Washington St, Louisville, 502-742-8315
www.butchertowngrocery.com/
CUISINE: American New/French
DRINKS: Full bar
SERVING: Lunch & Dinner; closed Mon & Tues
PRICE RANGE: $$
NEIGHBORHOOD: Butchertown

Set in a refurbished 19th-century building, this eatery offers a creative menu of American fare. Menu picks: Prince Edward Island Mussels and Cauliflower Steak. Great speakeasy vibe with great artisanal cocktails.

COALS ARTISAN PIZZA
3730 Frankfort Ave, Louisville, 502-742-8200
www.coalsartisanpizza.com
CUISINE: Pizza/Italian
DRINKS: Full Bar
SERVING: Lunch & Dinner
PRICE RANGE: $$
Here you'll find great pizza prepared in their coal-fired oven. Menu offers a great selection of pizzas with gourmet toppings and a selection of Italian classics. If you're a fan of having lots of meat on your pizza, this is the place for you. Especially savory is the Italian sausage stuffed with flavorful fennel and the spicy pepperoni. Great selection of wine and beers.

CON HUEVOS
2339 Frankfort Ave, Louisville, 502-384-3027
4938 US Hwy 42, Louisville, 502-384-3744
http://www.conhuevos.com/
CUISINE: Mexican
DRINKS: No Booze
SERVING: Breakfast & Lunch only, from 7 a.m.
PRICE RANGE: $$
NEIGHBORHOOD: 2 locations in Brownsboro & Holiday Manor

Mexican eatery (2 locations) with a fun interior with delightfully whimsical Mexican tiled floors, brick walls painted white, a few distressed wood furniture pieces. Street-side seating in good weather. Serves only breakfast and lunch. Favorites: Dulce de Leche French toast and
Mexican breakfast. Order and pay at counter then your meal is delivered to counter or table. Serving Cuban coffee.

DECCA
812 E Market St, Louisville, 502-749-8128
www.deccarestaurant.com
CUISINE: Southern, American
DRINKS: Full Bar
SERVING: Daily from 4:30, except Sunday, when it's closed
PRICE RANGE: $$$, sometimes $$$$
NEIGHBORHOOD: NuLu

Ingredient driven cuisine that makes creative use of locally available products. There's an outdoor area that's very nice, and a Cellar Lounge in the basement where you can get excellent craft cocktails and listen to live music. (Prices are steep when it comes to the drinks.) Upstairs, though, the food is spectacular: braised pork cheeks in black pepper Spaetzle, cauliflower and mission figs; shrimp a la plancha with chorizo and shaved fennel. There's a side I really liked, the savory cabbage a la plancha served with grain mustard and parsley sauce. (I could have made a meal of just that one dish.) Dessert? Get the strawberry and rhubarb cobbler.

DOC CROWS
127 West Main St, Louisville, 502-587-1626
www.doccrows.com
CUISINE: Southern, American
DRINKS: Full Bar
SERVING: Lunch, Dinner
PRICE RANGE: $$
NEIGHBORHOOD: Downtown
Also on Whiskey Row is this locals' favorite that is in the old Bonnie Brothers distillery dating back to the 1880s. This is also a popular watering hole as they offer over 160 whiskeys and over 100 bourbons and have an excellent wine list. Menu favorites include: Doc Chicken, Half Slab of Ribs, oysters on the half shell with bourbon mignonette and Carolina pulled pork.

THE EAGLE
1314 Bardstown Rd, Louisville, 502-498-8420
https://www.eaglerestaurant.com/
CUISINE: Southern/American (Traditional)
DRINKS: Full Bar
SERVING: Lunch & Dinner
PRICE RANGE: $$
NEIGHBORHOOD: Cherokee Triangle
Fun eatery featuring a lot of wooden accents in the interior and a big eagle painting on the brick wall. Lively bar scene with several beers on draft. Expansive outdoor area with seating at large picnic

tables. Menu carries Southern classics and comfort food. Known for their Fried Chicken, which you can order in quarters (choose white or dark meat), a half chicken or a whole. (They serve the chicken with a spicy hot honey concoction I'd never tasted before.) One of their appetizers is a sausage & kale dip that's interesting. Sides include spoonbread (a great dish I rarely see these days), white cheddar grits, and delicious mashed potatoes with a little horseradish whipped into it that gives it a delightful kick topped off with a savory gravy. Their homemade biscuits are served with a great blackberry jam and honey butter. Good selection of sandwiches and salads as well. (And they're all very good quality, not just a perfunctory nod to the menu category.)

ENGLISH GRILL
BROWN HOTEL
335 W Broadway, Louisville, 502-583-1234

www.brownhotel.com
This is the home of the original "Hot Brown," a sort of "baked sandwich," made with roasted turkey and toast points with a layer of Mornay sauce slopped over it all and topped with pecorino Romano cheese and bacon and tomatoes. People loved this concoction when it was first introduced in the 1920s and they've kept coming back for more. Of course, you can get this Louisville favorite in restaurants all over town, but it makes for a good story to tell your friends you ate it in the place where it was invented. When I'm here, however, I don't eat the Hot Brown (it's too filling for me). I go for the seared scallop Benedict (lamb bacon, quail egg and Béarnaise); or the crispy pork belly, served with Maker's Mark salted caramel candied apple and a Dijon trotter galette. The Hot Brown shouldn't overshadow the other great cuisine served here. This is one of the top 10 restaurants in town. Not the most *fun,* but certainly the best.

FEAST BBQ
909 E Market St, Ste 100, Louisville, 502-749-9900
www.feastbbq.com
CUISINE: Barbeque/American (Traditional)
DRINKS: Full Bar
SERVING: Lunch, Dinner
PRICE RANGE: $$
NEIGHBORHOOD: NuLu

Quaint little BBQ spot located in a former truck repair shop. Order up front and pay, then seat yourself at a picnic table while you wait for your order. Simple menu of BBQ, sides and drinks. Try the Country Boy Brewing Cougar Bait Ale, just one of the many local beers on tap. The weekends find this place packed with locals who come from miles around. Family friendly.

GARAGE BAR
700 E Market St, Louisville, 502-749-7100
www.garageonmarket.com
CUISINE: Pizza and more
DRINKS: Full Bar
SERVING: Dinner 7 nights; lunch on weekends
PRICE RANGE: $$
NEIGHBORHOOD: NuLu

The brick oven pizzas are the main attraction here. I should say "gourmet pizzas." The brick oven comes from Italy. Half the battle with pizza is won with the crust. They make their own here, using fresh yeast. They have their own "milled tomato" sauce, and that's the other half of the battle. Nice snacks like "rolled oysters," pork meatballs, boiled peanuts (a Southern tradition) and cauliflower salad. The country ham comes on a charcuterie board or on a pizza. The bar stocks some 25 to 30 specialty beers and a huge variety of rye and bourbon whiskeys from Kentucky.

GRIND BURGER KITCHEN
829 E. Market, Louisville, 502-213-0277
www.grindburgerkitchen.com
CUISINE: Burgers, Vegetarian
DRINKS: No Booze
SERVING: Lunch & dinner, Tues-Fri.
PRICE RANGE: $$
NEIGHBORHOOD: Preston
Liz and Jesse had run Louisville's favorite burger truck that traveled through the neighborhoods serving up some of the best hamburgers in the city made from local, grass-fed beef. The truck is gone, replaced with this brick-and-mortar eatery. You'll want to order the burger with 2 slices of Brie, thick-cut bacon and their special habanero jam that gives the thing a kick. Don't forget the essential side of fries.

HAMMERHEAD'S
921 Swan St, Louisville, 502-365-1112
www.louisvillehammerheads.com
CUISINE: Southern/American
DRINKS: Beer
SERVING: Dinner; closed Sundays
PRICE RANGE: $$
Small unique eatery offering a menu of pub grub including smoked meats (they use a double-barreled smoker for most of the meats served here), and vegetarian options. I'd get the "PBLT," which is a pork BLT, with generous cuts of smoked pork providing the delicious difference. Great variety of creatively conceived burgers, which explains why the lines start forming before they open at 5. No reservations, so get there early or go on a weekday.

HARVEST
624 E Market St, Louisville, 502-384-9090
www.harvestlouisville.com
CUISINE: Southern
DRINKS: Full Bar
SERVING: Lunch & Dinner daily except Monday, when it's closed
PRICE RANGE: $$ - $$$

Shiny wide-planked table tops and wooden chairs fill in the dining room here. Rustic but still clean and modern. Here the eggs come fresh from the farm. See that picture of the chicken farmer on the wall over there? He raised the chickens that laid those eggs you're eating. I've never been in a restaurant before where they put pictures on the wall of the farmers who raised the food. But the truth is that a lot of restaurants that claim to espouse a "farm to table" philosophy only take that concept as far as the lies written on the menu. (That "wild caught" salmon? It's really farm raised Atlantic salmon whose flesh would be gray instead of pink if they didn't dye the food they fed the poor fish. The grouper in that grouper sandwich? It's really farm-raised tilapia that cost a dollar a pound. That Dover sole? Give me a break.) Here at Harvest, though, they're serious. The proof is on the walls with the pictures of the people who raised the food. Most of what you eat here comes from within 100 miles of Louisville. The flour in which Coby Lee Ming dredges her fried chicken was milled in Kentucky. The chicken itself was raised on a nearby ranch. One of the best dishes here is the pork confit with jalapeño bacon grits; tomato melon gazpacho; the aforementioned excellent buttermilk fried chicken; sweet potato hummus; pork loin Milanese; a very tasty Burgoo (a Southern dish with chicken, pork, turkey, potatoes, corn, tomatoes and croutons). Desserts are just as good and just as creative.

JACK FRY'S
1007 Bardstown Rd, Louisville, 502-452-9244
www.jackfrys.com
CUISINE: American
DRINKS: Full Bar
SERVING: Breakfast, Lunch, Dinner
PRICE RANGE: $$$
NEIGHBORHOOD: Highlands- Cherokee Triangle
Some come for the music, others the food, and both deserve raves. This joint opened in 1933 and you'll wonder if they've ever renovated. It's got a warm Old South feel to it. You'll want to browse all the photos from the 1930s that decorate the walls. There are

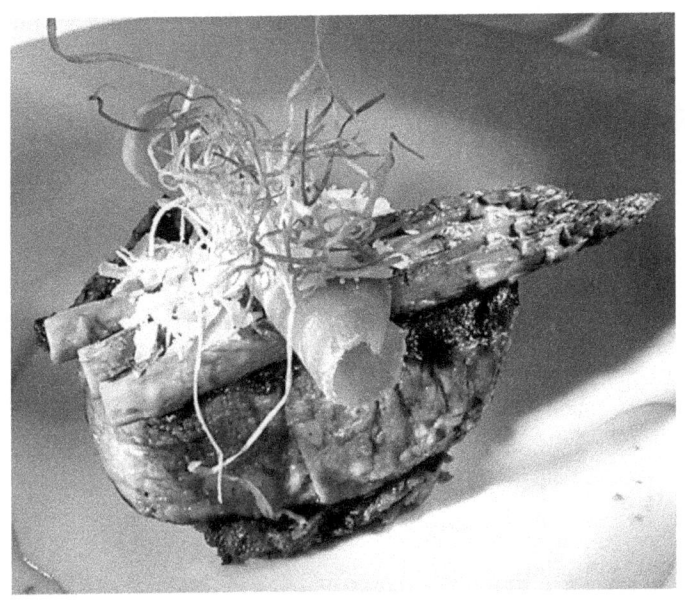

photos of the 1937 flood that swamped downtown. It was the damage done by this flood that instigated the development of the eastern parts of town that are now among the most upscale. The Southern inspired menu features favorites like beef filet, and scallops and winter melon. Great desserts like the Hazelnut torte. Live music every night (usually a piano player) with jazz on Monday, Friday & Saturday.

MAYAN CAFÉ
813 E Market St, Louisville, 502-566-0651
www.themayancafe.com
CUISINE: Mayan
DRINKS: Full Bar
SERVING: Lunch & Dinner weekdays; dinner only Saturday; closed Sunday
PRICE RANGE: $$
NEIGHBORHOOD: NuLu

Chef Bruce Ucan is from the Yucatan Peninsula, so he knows what's original and what's fake. Still, he adds a lot of twists to traditional Mexican fare in this simple and unpretentious place. Dishes like: black bean cakes; empanadas with chorizo, mozzarella and tomato-habanero sauce; oven-roasted rabbit with pumpkin seed mole and fried plantains; a burger made with grass-fed beef, bolillo bread, greens, pickled onions, tomatoes and Havarti cheese; *cochinita pibil*, or roasted pork. Flatbreads are served at lunch. There are numerous vegetarian dishes.

MILKWOOD
316 W. Main St, Louisville, 502-584-6455
www.milkwoodrestaurant.com
CUISINE: American, Comfort Food
DRINKS: Full Bar
SERVING: Dinner nightly except Monday, when it's closed.
PRICE RANGE: $$$
NEIGHBORHOOD: Downtown

Top Chef and Iron Chef Edward Lee's newest venture, located in the basement at **Actors Theater of Louisville**, is a celebration of Southern cuisine with Asian ingredients. He calls it "a southern speakeasy with an Asian pantry." Korean Lee came from New York to see the Derby one year and well, the rest is history. Menu favorites include: Miso Smothered Chicken, Crispy Skin Duck, fried chicken & waffles with Korean chili, collard greens with kimchi and Teras Major steak. This elegant eatery seats approximately 100 and is ideal for pre- or after theater dining.

MUSSEL & BURGER BAR
113 South 7th St, Louisville, 502-749-6451
9200 Taylorsville Rd, Louisville, 502-384-4834
https://www.mussel-burger-bar.com/
CUISINE: Mussels / Burgers / American (Traditional)
DRINKS: Full Bar
SERVING: Lunch & Dinner
PRICE RANGE: $$
NEIGHBORHOOD: 2 locations – Downtown & East End

Popular bistro with a vintage décor and lots of wood, from the ceiling to the floor to the chairs to the big wooden back-bar, relieved a little by the banquettes and the slender white columns painted a stark white to offer some contrast against the otherwise dark interior. Has a very different menu of American fare with some nods to Europe. While the different offerings of mussels are certainly a draw (get them served as Moules Basquaise (with chorizo, olive oil, lobster broth), Greek style, Meuniere (white wine, shallots, garlic, butter), Curry Cream, Blue Cheese Beer or Mexican Pozole), the great selection of burgers (probably 14 to 16 creative iterations) almost certainly draws an even larger crowd of patrons. Favorites: Blue Cheese Beer Mussels; Spanish Blue Burger (La Peral Spanish blue cheese & fig marmalade). They also serve a variety of salads, sandwiches and the sides bear a close look. Great cocktails.

PROOF ON MAIN
21C MUSEUM HOTEL
702 West Main St, Louisville, 502-217-6360
www.proofonmain.com
CUISINE: Contemporary American
DRINKS: Full Bar
SERVING: Breakfast, Lunch & Dinner
PRICE RANGE: $$$$
NEIGHBORHOOD: Downtown
I already wrote about what a fabulous environment this place enjoys because it's located in the 21c Museum Hotel. Charred octopus; garlic risotto; Woodland Farm's hog chop; scallops served with corn bread, country ham, asparagus, gremolata and sorghum; bison burger with smoked bacon and Tillamook cheddar. For something different, try the Kentucky trout tartare. Almost everything served here is locally sourced. The bar's a great place to hang out.

Both places are bright airy rooms with lots of art decorating the walls.

ROYALS HOT CHICKEN
736 E Market St, Louisville, 502-919-7068
www.royalschicken.com/
CUISINE: American Traditional
DRINKS: Full bar
SERVING: Lunch & Dinner; closed Sunday
PRICE RANGE: $$
NEIGHBORHOOD: NuLu
Known for their great Nashville Hot Fried Chicken. Modern, spacious eatery with a creative menu of traditional American fare. Nice selection of beers and delicious creative shakes (try the bourbon shake). Counter service.

RYE
900 E Market St, Louisville, 502-749-6200
www.ryeonmarket.com
CUISINE: Contemporary American
DRINKS: Full Bar
SERVING: Dinner nightly from 5
PRICE RANGE: $$$
NEIGHBORHOOD: NuLu
A brick wall on the right side of the bar and ceilings painted black give the place a cozy, intimate feeling. In the restaurant section, it's the ubiquitous bare wooden tables and chairs, all no-nonsense, but that's Louisville for you. This is a great place to eat at the bar if you're by yourself. The bartenders really know their stuff. They have a streamlined but excellent whiskey list. The food is very good here and Rye

attracts a lot of hipsters (especially the bar scene). They have 3 or 4 kinds of oysters (Fanny Bay, Winnow, Chincoteague), which I didn't find a lot of elsewhere in Louisville. Also a kale salad with sorghum dressing that's really good. Menu highlights: Braised Berkshire pork served with yellow grits; a lobster fettuccini that I just had to have, with English peas and arugula, Parmesan and hazelnut; a strip steak with green peppercorn Bordelaise and crispy leeks; a whole roasted silk snapper served with French green lentils, kale, capers and lemon.

THE SILVER DOLLAR
1761 Frankfort Ave, Louisville, (502) 259-9540
www.whiskeybythedrink.com
CUISINE: Gastropub, Southern
DRINKS: Full Bar

SERVING: Brunch, Dinner, Late night
PRICE RANGE: $$
NEIGHBORHOOD: Crescent Hills
This gastropub located in a former red brick firehouse is a celebration of an old 1950s Bakersfield, California, honky-tonk serving great Southern dishes like Chicken Fried Steak, Breaded Catfish, and Fried Chicken Livers. The bar serves Kentucky bourbon and rye whiskeys and is home to some interesting craft cocktails. There's also an incredible list of beers.

TACO LUCHADOR
938 Baxter Ave, Louisville, 502-583-0440
5202 New Cut Rd, Louisville, 502-384-8457
500 W Jefferson St, Louisville, 502-409-9254
9204 Taylorsville Rd, Louisville, 502-708-1675
112 Meridian Av, Louisville, 502-709-5154
https://www.el-taco-luchador.com/
CUISINE: Tacos
DRINKS: Full Bar
SERVING: Lunch & Dinner
PRICE RANGE: $$
NEIGHBORHOOD: several locations
I love the startling yellow bar seats here in this small Mexican joint. They and their yellow table chair counterparts are that Mexican color used by Fiestaware in the 1960s. (They are blue in a different location.) Plenty of outdoor seating as well. Counter eatery serving tacos, tortas, nachos, and sandwiches, all very high quality. Frozen margaritas.

WAGNER'S PHARMACY
3113 S Fourth St, Louisville, 502-375-3800

www.wagnerspharmacy.com
CUISINE: American, Burgers
DRINKS: No Booze
SERVING: Breakfast, Brunch
PRICE RANGE: $$
NEIGHBORHOOD: South Louisville
This is a shrine for those who love the Kentucky Derby with horse racing memorabilia pasted all over the walls. When you walk in here, it's like walking through a time machine because the place doesn't look like it's changed much since it opened in 1922. It's a pharmacy with an all-American diner serving burgers and such. It's not the food that's the attraction. Go the day after the Derby and meet the trainers and jockeys that lost the race the day before. Since it's located right outside Churchill Downs, the place is always crawling with trainers, jockeys, groomsmen, track workers and betters. Be sure to look over the photos of past legends who used to frequent the place.

WILD EGGS
121 S Floyd St, Louisville, 502-690-5925
153 English Station Rd, Louisville, 502-618-3449
1311 Herr Lane, Louisville, 502-618-2905
3985 Dutchmans Lane, Louisville, 502-893-8005
https://wildeggs.com/
CUISINE: Breakfast/American (New)
DRINKS: No Booze
SERVING: Breakfast & Lunch
PRICE RANGE: $$
NEIGHBORHOOD: several locations

This may be a "chain" restaurant, but they succeed in bringing the high quality and creative attention to details to a simple-enough breakfast-focused concept that you expect to find when you go to a "fine dining" restaurant. The staff is smart & friendly (as opposed to dull-witted & surly you often find in so many breakfast-only joints) and the food of the highest quality, from the fresh-squeezed orange juice to the homemade cinnamon bun (with croissant style bread stuffed with butter, brown sugar & cinnamon, cooked in a cast iron skillet and topped with sweet vanilla bean icing). While the focus is on breakfast (with crepes, omelets, several Benedict selections, pancakes, waffles, French toast), they also have high quality sandwiches, salads and soups. Favorites: Sweet Home Apple Bourbon Crepes; Chicken crepes with a side of pancakes; Build Your Own Omelet (with a wide selection of fillings); Jimmy the Greek Frittata; the Hash Brown Casserole is a side dish you'll go nuts over.

WILTSHIRE BAKERY & CAFE
901 Barret Ave, Louisville, 502-581-8561
www.wiltshirepantry.com/bakery-and-cafe
CUISINE: Breakfast/Brunch
DRINKS: Beer & Wine Only
SERVING: Breakfast & Lunch; closed Mondays
PRICE RANGE: $
The black-and-white chalkboard menu gives this combination bakery and café offering a great bakery counter with a wide selection of pastries, artisanal breads and brioche a homey, small-town feeling. Café offers breakfast and light lunch fare. They have a

homemade "fried apple pie," kind of their take on a Pop Tart, but in much better flavors. Or get their Croque Monsieur with savory ham and melted Gruyere cheese served atop their homemade brioche.

WILTSHIRE ON MARKET
636 E Market St, Louisville, 502-589-5224
www.wiltshirepantry.com
CUISINE: American (New)
DRINKS: Full Bar
SERVING: Dinner; Thurs - Sun
PRICE RANGE: $$
Popular eatery offering a great dining experience and top-notch cocktails. Creative menu includes dishes like: Smoked Alligator Tacos and Beef Pave & potato onion cakes. Expansive cocktail menu.

YUMMY POLLO
4222-B Bishop Lane, Louisville, 502-618-1400
http://yummypollo.com/
CUISINE: Peruvian/Latin American
DRINKS: No Booze
SERVING: Lunch & Dinner, Closed on Sunday
PRICE RANGE: $
NEIGHBORHOOD: Hayfield Dundee
Very basic Peruvian eatery where chicken is the king (their slogan). Peruvian style charcoal fired rotisserie chicken is their specialty. (High quality naturally raised hormone-free chickens.) That and their tasty side dishes (get their cilantro lime rice) is all there is to it, but it's more finger-licking good than "You Know Where." Order at counter and eat at one of the handful of tables provided or get it to go. Outdoor

seating is nothing to brag about. You're sitting on the sidewalk next to the parking lot. No, the décor is nothing. The food everything. And it's cheap.

Chapter 5
NIGHTLIFE

BARDSTOWN ROAD

Down the 2-mile long Bardstown – Baxter Avenue Corridor there are something like 40 bars, some of then located in dumpy little dives and others in fancy upscale restaurants. But it's the best place to spend an evening bar hopping. Besides the bars, you'll find a captivating collection of galleries, shops, antique stores, artisans selling crafts and tourist traps selling cheap merchandise. But it's great fun.

HOLY GRALE
1034 Bardstown Rd, Louisville, 502-459-9939
www.holygralelouisville.com
NEIGHBORHOOD: Bardstown Road
NEIGHBORHOOD: Bardstown Road / Highlands
Formerly a Unitarian Church dating back to 1905, this dark and cozy Victorian structure in the Highlands neighborhood is now a gathering place for those who worship the international beers (some of them quite rare) served at Holy Grale. The bar features over 25 taps and an impressive bottle list. The bar menu is good, with things like Pork Belly Sliders and Chorizo Tacos. Try to run up to the loft

where the choir used to sing just so you can see the original stained-glass windows.

MAGNOLIA BAR & GRILL
1398 S 2nd St, Louisville, 502-637-9052
www.magbarlouisville.com
This popular dive bar fills up for late night action. The name "grill" is misleading as no food is served here. There is a small concert stage however, the music is generally provided by a jukebox or a DJ playing EDM music on Wednesday nights, when drinks are even cheaper. (Sunday they do a Bingo Night.)

META
425 W Chestnut St, Louisville, 502-822-6382
www.metalouisville.com
Located in downtown Louisville, this upscale speakeasy-themed bar specializes in craft and classic cocktails in an atmosphere that takes you back in

time: penny-tiled floors, handpainted wallpaper. Speaking of "classic," if you've never had the classic Sidecar, you'll get a good one here.

NOWHERE BAR
1133 Bardstown Rd, Louisville, 502-451-0466
www.nowherelouisville.com
Gay video and dance bar that pumps electronic dance music all night. If you're not into dancing there's lots of TVs, pool tables and an outdoor patio. Many theme nights with DJs, karaoke, and trivia.

OLD SEELBACH BAR
SEELBACH HILTON HOTEL
500 Fourth Ave, Louisville, 502-585-3200
www.seelbachhilton.com
You have to stop in here for a drink. Just one at least, if only to walk through the majestic lobby of this grand hotel with its marble columns, coffered ceilings and rich wood finishes. Scott Fitzgerald, before he

wrote "The Great Gatsby," used to hang out in this bar when he was stationed in Louisville as a second lieutenant. Fitzgerald long ago drank himself into oblivion, but you're still here. Why not try a "bourbon tasting"? You get 4 one-ounce pours for about $20.

THE SILVER DOLLAR
1761 Frankfort Ave, Louisville, 502-259-9540
www.whiskeybythedrink.com
NEIGHBORHOOD: Crescent Hills
A great hangout for the bourbon and whiskey connoisseur. This former fire house with its red brick walls makes a good place to enjoy the 100-odd whiskeys on offer. They have a large collection of vinyl, and play music from the likes of Merle Haggard and other country rock singers from the 1950s that personified the Bakersfield sound.

ZANZABAR
2100 South Preston St, Louisville, 502-635-9227
www.zanzabarlouisville.com
NEIGHBORHOOD: Schnitzelburg
This is a small music venue and dive bar but it's also a full service restaurant serving Southern cuisine. Live music schedule features everything from traveling punk bands to popular Louisville bands. The food is good and they even have some great vintage video games.

Chapter 6
WHAT TO SEE & DO

ACTORS THEATER OF LOUISVILLE
316 West Main St, Louisville, 502-584-1205
www.actorstheatre.org
This theatre is recognized nationally for its achievements in the arts and critically acclaimed productions. The company presents original and classic theater works. Plays that premiere here go on to tour the world. Pulitzer Prizes have been awarded to "dinner with Friends" and "Crimes of the Heart," both of which originated here. The **Humana Festival of New American Plays** runs in the spring.

BIG FOUR BRIDGE
1101 River Rd., Louisville,
www.louisvillewaterfront.com/projects/big_four/
HOURS: 6 a.m. – 11 p.m.
ADMISSION: No fee
NEIGHBORHOOD: Downtown/Waterfront
The Big Four Bridge is a six-span former railroad truss bridge that crosses the Ohio River, connecting Louisville with Jeffersonville in Indiana. It was completed in 1895, and updated in 1929. You can walk across it in 10 minutes.

BUFFALO TRACE DISTILLERY
113 Great Buffalo Trace, Frankfort, 502-696-5926
www.buffalotracedistillery.com
HOURS: 9 – 5; Thurs – Sat.
ADMISSION: No fee
Popular for tourists and locals, the tour begins with a video and then winds through a path of rolling bourbon barrels offering a behind-the-scenes peek at a distillery in action. Visitors get to taste some of the award-winning products. Reservations only needed for large groups. Tours last approximately 1 hour.

CAVE HILL CEMETERY
701 Baxter Ave, Louisville, 502-451-5630
www.cavehillcemetery.com
Col. Harlan Sanders of Kentucky Fried Chicken fame is buried here. So is George Rogers Clark, who founded Louisville. (He was the brother of William Clark, who formed the Clark part of the Lewis & Clark Expedition.) Tours are available. This 296-acre Victorian era National Cemetery and arboretum are open daily. The stunning landscaping and massive trees are just as impressive as the marble and granite headstones. Whether you're a Civil War buff or a garden enthusiast, this is a must-see. Over 5,000 soldiers are buried here, a large number of them dating back to the Civil War. Listed on the National Register of Historic Places, this is the largest cemetery in the area. The cemetery is the site of natural rock outcroppings and hilly topography and features ponds, statuary, and architecturally elegant

tombs. The cemetery boasts more than 500 kinds of trees and garden plants growing in the gardens that you will find it a beautiful getaway from the busy Highlands neighborhood nearby.

CHEROKEE PARK
745 Cochran Hill Rd, Louisville, 502-574-7275
https://louisvilleky.gov/government/parks/park-list/cherokee-park
Designed in 1891 by Frederick Law Olmsted (some people consider the work he did in Louisville to be even greater than his work on Central Park or Brooklyn's Prospect Park), this 409-acre park is listed as the 69th most popular municipal park in the country. Beargrass Creek runs though the park, crossed by many pedestrian and automobile bridges. Park features include: a 2.4 mile scenic loop with separate lanes for traffic and bikes.

CHURCHILL DOWNS
700 Central Ave, Louisville, 502-636-4400
www.churchilldowns.com
This racetrack is known worldwide as the annual host for 3-year-old thoroughbreds running in the Kentucky Derby. If you don't want to put up with the insane crowds on Derby Day, attend one of the other race days when there is no hassle. You'll get to roam around the storied track for a small fee. In the lobby there's the **Kentucky Derby Museum**, which is a lot of fun. (This track officially opened in 1875, the same year as the first Kentucky Derby.) This track is rated the 5th in America and has a capacity of 120,000 people.

COPPER & KINGS
1121 E Washington St, Louisville, 502-561-0267
http://www.copperandkings.com/
HOURS: 10 a.m. – 4 p.m.

ADMISSION: Minimal fee
NEIGHBORHOOD: Butchertown
Distillery that crafts untraditional distilled Pure Pot-still brandies. Tours offered 10 a.m. – 3 p.m. on the hours. Thurs – Mon. Rooftop tasting with breathtaking view of Louisville skyline. Reservations recommended.

EVAN WILLIAMS BOURBON EXPERIENCE
528 W Main St, Louisville, 502-272-2623
http://evanwilliams.com/visit.php
HOURS: Open daily
ADMISSION: Minimal admission fee
NEIGHBORHOOD: Downtown/West Main
Located on Louisville's historic "Whiskey Row" featuring an artisanal distillery, guided tours, and educational Bourbon tastings (if you can call it that!). Learn the history of Kentucky's first commercial distiller and the history of Kentucky's native spirit.

FALLS OF THE OHIO
201 W Riverside Dr, Clarksville, 812-280-9970
www.fallsoftheohio.org/
HOURS: 7 a.m. – 11 p.m.
ADMISSION: Nominal fee plus parking
NEIGHBORHOOD: Ohio River
Located on the banks of the Ohio River, this State Park is home to 390-million-year-old fossil beds. Park activities include: fishing, hiking, walking, fossil viewing, bird watching, and picnicking.

KENTUCKY CENTER FOR THE ARTS
501 West Main St, Louisville, 502-584-7777

www.kentuckycenter.org
This Center houses some of the city's major arts organizations and offers an impressive roster of music, dance, theater and other events. Home to The **Louisville Orchestra**, **Kentucky Opera**, **Louisville Ballet**, **Stage One** and PNC Bank Broadway Across America.

KENTUCKY DERBY MUSEUM
704 Central Ave, Louisville, 502-637-1111
www.derbymuseum.org
My first time in Louisville was not to attend the Derby. But my first stop when I got settled was still Churchill Downs because of this museum. Located on the front steps of historic Churchill Downs, this museum is one of Louisville's premiere attractions. Here you can learn all about the Kentucky Derby any time during the year. The two level museum features exhibits that celebrate thoroughbred racing and the Kentucky Derby – known as the first jewel in racing's Triple Crown. Here you can mount a fake horse and "ride it" for the same 2 minutes it takes to run in the Derby. There's also a hi-def film shown in on a 360-degree screen that takes you through the history of the

Derby, which was first run here in 1785, the year the track first opened. Take one of the "backside" tours to the barn areas where a thousand horses live during the racing meet. When there is no racing, other tours take you into Churchill Downs and you get to go to places casual visitors never see.

LOUISVILLE GLASSWORKS
815 West Market St, Louisville, 502-992-3270

www.louisvilleglassworks.com
This unique center of glassworks offers what they like to label as "edutainment" opportunities. Visitors get to enjoy the walk-in workshop, tours, flameworking experiences and the gallery that exhibits flameworked glass, flat glass and jewelry fashioned by some 30 artists. Glassworks facilities include: a hot shop, a welding shop, a glass gallery and a gift shop. The newest addition is the "Flame Your Own Snowman" workshop where guests can work with artist Mark Payton to create their own snowman. Daily tours available for a nominal fee.

LOUISVILLE HISTORIC TOURS
1212 S 4th St, Louisville, 502-718-2764
http://louisvillehistorictours.com/
HOURS: 11 a.m. – 9:30 p.m. daily;
ADMISSION: Modest fee ($20 pp)
NEIGHBORHOOD: Old Louisville
These 90 – minute walking tours are led by a knowledgeable tour guide through the streets of Louisville passing a variety of historic homes, big and small, from Victorian style to Romanesque. Reservations recommended.

LOUISVILLE SLUGGER MUSEUM
800 West Main St, Louisville, 877-775-8443
www.sluggermuseum.com
You can't miss the 120-foot high baseball bat outside this place on Main Street. You can visit the main lobby for free. In this lobby is the **Signature Wall**, where you'll find 8,000-plus signatures of players who signed contracts to use the famous bat. If you

pay admission to the museum, you get a tour of the factory where bats are made that are used by many Major League players. (You'll smell the maple and white ash woods used to make the bats.) And actually handle bats once used by Cal Ripken, Jr., and Mickey Mantle. (For a fee, they'll even make a bat with your name on it as a souvenir.) Outside is the **Louisville Slugger Walk of Fame**, which runs a mile from the museum down to the city's minor-league ball park. You'll pass by bronze monuments and plaques documenting such baseball greats as Ty Cobb and Babe Ruth. I love baseball, so this is all great fun for me.

MINT JULEP TOURS
502-583-1433
www.mintjuleptours.com
They offer a Bourbon Trail Tour that takes you out to the distilleries to see how bourbon is made first-hand. But they also offer Louisville city tours (the city's only real comprehensive tour), horse country tours and culinary tours.

MUHAMMAD ALI CENTER
144 North Sixth St, Louisville, 502-584-9254
https://alicenter.org
The Center offers three levels of award-winning exhibitions and galleries celebrating the life and career of Muhammad Ali. The museum features many interactive and multimedia exhibits. (Go ahead and try your hand at the speed bag.) The Center is also known for its programming that serves people of all cultures, ages, nationalities, and geographic areas.

MUSEUM ROW ON MAIN
Main St, Louisville
www.museumrowonmain.com
Museum Row consists of nine original galleries or museums located within four walkable blocks on Main Street. The venues include: 21C Museum Hotel, Frazier History Museum, Glassworks, Kentucky Center for the Performing Arts, Kentucky Museum of Art & Craft, KentuckyShow!, Louisville Science

Center, Louisville Slugger Museum & Factory, and Muhammad Ali Center. Check website for events.

OHIO RIVER
Thomas Jefferson called the Ohio River "the most beautiful river on earth." This river marks Kentucky's northern border and the normally gentle river breaks its smooth run with the Falls of the Ohio, a 2.2-mile-long limestone rapids. Here the river drops 23.9 feet.

OLD LOUISVILLE
North of the University of Louisville main campus is the section of town called Old Louisville, and it runs to the southern border of downtown. Expect to see lots of stately Victorian homes tucked in on both sides of gorgeous tree-lined streets. Where once the elite lived in the 19th Century, like a lot of such sections, the 20th Century was not kind to it and it got really rundown and awful, but gentrification has brought it back big-time. Well worth the time.

SPEED ART MUSEUM
2035 S 3rd St, Louisville, 502-634-2700
www.speedmuseum.org/
HOURS: 10 a.m. – 5 p.m.; Noon – 5 p.m. on Sun; Closed Mondays
ADMISSION: Nominal fee
NEIGHBORHOOD: University
Originally known as the J.B. Speed Memorial Museum, this is the oldest, largest, and most acclaimed museum of art in Kentucky. Museum offers modern architecture, inventive programming, interactive exhibits, and a variety of "art

experiences." Museum offers weekly events, the Speed Concert Series, an Interactive Family gallery, and a popular late-night event called Art After Dark. Museum houses a collection of African art, ancient art, Native American art, American art, European art, and contemporary art. Arts represented include: Rembrandt, Rubens, Monet, Rodin, Gainsborough, Picasso, Cezanne, Matisse, and modern works by artists such as Chuck Close and Frank Stella.

SWANSON CONTEMPORARY
638 East Market St, Louisville, 502-589-5466
www.swansoncontemporary.com
Located in the East Market Gallery District (now called "**NuLu**," for "New Louisville"), which has been gentrified and is now filled with interesting places, this being one of them: a gallery that showcases contemporary national and regional artists focusing on works in video, installation, photography,

conceptual art, painting, performance, and sculpture. This gallery mounts ten exhibitions annually on the main level with a lower level video and installation space and outdoor sculpture garden.

WHISKEY ROW
This is a block-long stretch from 101-133 W. Main Street that once served as home to the bourbon industry in Louisville, Kentucky. The collection of Revivalist and Chicago School-style buildings with cast-iron storefronts were built between 1852 and 1905. On a list of Louisville Most Endangered Historic Places, the buildings were slated for demolition in 2011, but some quick-thinking people worked up an agreement among the city, local developers, and preservationists that saved Whiskey Row.

WATERFRONT PARK
River Rd, Louisville, 502-574-3768
Popular 85-acre park adjacent to downtown Louisville and the Ohio River. Landscaped for

optimum usage with paths for running and biking. Lots of family activities. Equipped with picnic tables, benches, and playgrounds, a lot of this park overlooks the Ohio River, giving it an added dimension. The park's Great Lawn is like a massive front yard for the city, and is site of many events including Thunder Over Louisville, Derby Festival and Forecastle Festival. Here you'll also find the **Big Four Bridge**, a former railroad bridge connecting Louisville and Jeffersonville, Ind., that was redesigned as a pedestrian walkway and cycling route.

ZEPHYR GALLERY
610 East Market St, Louisville, 502-585-5646
www.zephyrgallery.org

This multidisciplinary exhibition space is an artist-run initiative that offers proposal-based exhibitions and collaborations.

Chapter 7
SHOPPING & SERVICES

CARMICHAEL'S BOOKSTORE
1295 Bardstown Rd, Louisville, 502-456-6950
www.carmichaelsbookstore.com

This is Louisville's oldest indie bookstore featuring shelf after shelf of new and old titles. Visit the website for a schedule of upcoming events and book signings, authors' readings, etc.

CITY CONCIERGE
www.cityconciergelouisville.com
Online personal concierge service that is tailored to each clients needs and interests. Get information and access for nightclubs and local events. Tips o shopping, services, galleries, and shopping.

COLLECTIONS
Westport Village, 1301 Herr Ln # 181, Louisville, 502-749-7200
https://shopcollectionscloset.com
Collections, a locally run fashion boutique, provides a variety of fashions for women of all ages. The boutique features everything from handbags to shoes, faux leather slacks, snazzy party dresses and lots more. It may be located in a strip mall, but don't let that put you off. Lots of treasures inside this place.

FOURTH STREET LIVE
411 S 4th St, Louisville, 502-584-7170
www.4thstlive.com
This is an urban mall with a variety of stores and restaurants. Restaurants include: T.G.I. Fridays, Hard Rock Café, and RiRa Irish Pub. Nightlife venues include: PBR Louisville A Cowboy Bar, The Marquee Bar, Kill Devil Club and Howl at the Moon. The food court also has chain restaurants like Philly Station, Wendy's, Subway, KFC, and Taco Bell. Retail outlets include: CVS, Foot Locker, and T-Mobile.

HEINE BROTHERS' COFFEE
1250 Bardstown Rd, Louisville, 502-456-5108
www.heinebroscoffee.com
Heine Brothers has great coffee. This is a great place to have a seat outside after you've bought a book at **Carmichael's** just adjacent. **SEVERAL LOCATIONS IN THE LOUISVILLE AREA.**

LOUISVILLE BEER STORE
746 East Market, Louisville, 502- 569-2337
www.louisvillebeerstore.com
NEIGHBORHOOD: NuLu
It sounds kind of strange to think of a "beer store," but that's what it is. A huge selection of artisanal and craft beers. They have 8 beers on tap (rotating). Beer merchandise, gift sets, glassware. Beer tastings and flights. A great little place.

PLEASE & THANK YOU
800 E Market St, Louisville, 502-533-0113
www.pleaseandthankyoulouisville.com
NEIGHBORHOOD: NuLu
A bakery that has such popular chocolate chip cookies that they created a "baking kit" so you can make them at home. (They won't reveal the exact recipe.) Great coffees, bagels, scones, brownies, other baked goods. Good coffees and teas. They have great paninis: a breakfast version made with local eggs, basil pesto, mozzarella on focaccia; there's also cinnamon toast, actually, a brioche topped with butter, cinnamon and sugar. Oh, God, does that take me back to my youth. Peanut butter toast, too.

REVELRY BOUTIQUE GALLERY
742 E Market St, Louisville, 502-414-1278
www.revelrygallery.com/

NEIGHBORHOOD: NuLu
Beautiful shop filled with revolving selection of handmade goods curated by the owner. A super selection of jewelry, home décor, art, home goods, and other creative items made by local artisans.

RODES
4938 Brownsboro Rd, Louisville, 502-753-7633
www.rodes.com
NEIGHBORHOOD: Brownsboro
Since 1914, this has been a popular shopping destination offering the best men's and women's apparel. Get a seersucker suit and a Panama hat. The men's shop has two in-shop boutiques featuring Ermenegildo Zegna and Eton of Sweden collections. For the ladies, there's an eclectic selection of designer fashions including shoes, handbags, jewelry, scarves, and skin care products. (And they have a big selection of hats you'll need for Derby Day.)

INDEX

2

21C MUSEUM HOTEL, 9, 37

6

610 MAGNOLIA, 19

8

8UP, 20

A

Actors Theater of Louisville, 35
ACTORS THEATER OF LOUISVILLE, 52
American, 30
American (New), 20, 43
American New, 21
American Traditional, 38

B

Bardstown Road, 7

Big Four Bridge, 66
BIG FOUR BRIDGE, 53
BLUE DOG BAKERY & CAFÉ, 20
Breakfast, 21, 42
BRECKINRIDGE INN, 10
BRENDON'S CATCH 23, 21
BROWN HOTEL, 11, 26
Brunch, 42
BUFFALO TRACE DISTILLERY, 53
BUTCHERTOWN GROCERY, 21

C

Cafe, 21
CARMICHAEL'S BOOKSTORE, 69
CAVE HILL CEMETERY, 54
CHEROKEE PARK, 55
CHURCHILL DOWNS, 56
CITY CONCIERGE, 70
COALS ARTISAN PIZZA, 22
COLLECTIONS, 70
CON HUEVOS, 23
COPPER & KINGS, 56

D

DECCA, 24
DOC CROWS, 25
DUPONT MANSION BED & BREAKFAST, 12

E

EAGLE, 25
EMBASSY SUITES BY HILTON, 12
English Grill, 11

ENGLISH GRILL, 26
EVAN WILLIAMS BOURBON EXPERIENCE, 57

F

FALLS OF THE OHIO, 57
FEAST BBQ, 27
FOURTH STREET LIVE, 71
French, 21

G

GALT HOUSE, 13
GARAGE BAR, 28
GRIND BURGER KITCHEN, 29

H

HAMMERHEAD'S, 30
HAMPTON INN LOUISVILLE, 13
HARVEST, 31
HEINE BROTHERS' COFFEE, 72
Highlands, 7
HOLY GRALE, 46
Hot Brown, 11
Humana Festival of New American Plays, 52
HYATT REGENCY LOUISVILLE, 13

I

INN AT WOODHAVEN, 14
Italian, 22

J

JACK FRY'S, 32

K

KENTUCKY CENTER FOR THE ARTS, 57
KENTUCKY DERBY MUSEUM, 58
Kentucky Opera, 58

L

Louisville Ballet, 58
LOUISVILLE BEER STORE, 72
LOUISVILLE GLASSWORKS, 59
LOUISVILLE HISTORIC TOURS, 60
Louisville Orchestra, 58
LOUISVILLE SLUGGER MUSEUM, 60
Lyft, 8

M

MAGNOLIA BAR & GRILL, 47
MAYAN CAFÉ, 34
META, 47
MILKWOOD, 35
MINT JULEP TOURS, 61
MUHAMMAD ALI CENTER, 62
MUSEUM ROW ON MAIN, 62
MUSSEL AND BURGER BAR, 36

N

NOWHERE BAR, 48

NuLu, 64

O

OHIO RIVER, 63
OLD LOUISVILLE, 63
OLD SEELBACH BAR, 48

P

Pizza, 22
PLEASE & THANK YOU, 73
PROOF ON MAIN, 37

R

REVELRY BOUTIQUE GALLERY, 73
RODES, 74
ROYALS HOT CHICKEN, 38
RYE, 38

S

Seafood, 21
SEELBACH HOTEL, 15, 48
SILVER DOLLAR, 39, 49
Southern, 30
SPEED ART MUSEUM, 63
Stage One, 58
STAYBRIDGE SUITES LOUISVILLE EAST, 16
Steakhouse, 21
SWANSON REED CONTEMPORARY, 64

T

TACO LUCHADOR, 40

TARC, 8

U

Uber, 8

W

WAGNER'S PHARMACY, 40
WATERFRONT PARK, 65
WHISKEY ROW, 65
WILD EGGS, 41

WILTSHIRE BAKERY & CAFE, 42
WILTSHIRE ON MARKET, 43

Y

YUMMY POLLO, 43

Z

ZANZABAR, 50
ZEPHYR GALLERY, 66

Other Books by the Same Author

Andrew Delaplaine has written in widely varied fields: screenplays, novels (adult and juvenile), travel writing, journalism. His books are available in quality bookstores, libraries, as well as all online retailers.

JACK HOUSTON ST. CLAIR POLITICAL THRILLERS

On Election night, as China and Russia mass soldiers on their common border in preparation for war, there's a tie in the Electoral College that forces the decision for President into the House of Representatives as mandated by the Constitution. The incumbent Republican President, working through his Aide for Congressional Liaison, uses the Keystone File, which contains dirt on every member of Congress, to blackmail members into supporting the Republican candidate. The action runs from Election Night in November to Inauguration Day on January 20. Jack Houston St. Clair runs a small detective agency in Miami. His father is Florida Governor Sam Houston St. Clair, the Republican candidate. While he tries to help his dad win the election, Jack also gets hired to follow up on some suspicious wire transfers involving drug smugglers, leading him to a sunken narco-sub off Key West that has $65 million in cash in its hull.

AFTER THE OATH: DAY ONE
AFTER THE OATH: MARCH WINDS
WEDDING AT THE WHITE HOUSE

Only three months have passed since Sam Houston St. Clair was sworn in as the new President, but a lot has happened. Returning from Vienna where he met with Russian and Chinese diplomats, Sam is making his way back to Flagler Hall in Miami, his first trip home since being inaugurated. Son Jack is in the midst of turmoil of his own back in Miami, dealing with various dramas, not the least of which is his increasing alienation from Babylon Fuentes and his growing attraction to the seductive Lupe Rodriguez. Fernando Pozo addresses new problems as he struggles to expand Cuba's secret operations in the U.S., made even more difficult as U.S.-Cuban relations thaw. As his father returns home, Jack knows Sam will find as much trouble at home as he did in Vienna.

www.ingramcontent.com/pod-product-compliance
Lightning Source LLC
Chambersburg PA
CBHW071740040426
42446CB00012B/2412